Bled, n. French and colloquial Arabic, *bled*, representing *balad*, vast stretch of country or *bilad*, land, country.

In parts of North Africa formerly under French rule: an uncultivated wasteland; the hinterland behind a fertile, populated area. Also, in extended use: a rolling plain or other open stretch of land.

Published by Factory Hollow Press

Factory Hollow Press
Amherst, Massachusetts

www.factoryhollowpress.com

Design by Pam Glaven, Impress, Northampton, MA
Printed by The Studley Press, Dalton, MA

2ND PRINTING, 2011

ISBN 978-0-9840698-7-3
Copyright © 2010 by Frances McCue

FOR GARY GREAVES

CONTENTS

Like This For Years – 9
Split Sky – 11
Seeing Is Believing – 13
Into The Box – 14
My Difficult Home – 16
Slight, Then Swoon – 17
The Lilt, The Toppling Over – 19
The Bled – 20
Wings Installed – 22
Dying In Three Languages – 23
I Should Say – 27
Three Ways of Longing – 28
Kinship – 29
Trio Down One – 30
Console, Preacher, Console – 32
Problems With Clothes – 34
Pinning on Wings – 35
After the Bled, On To The Shoals – 37
The Patient Saint – 38
In The Space – 40
You Could Know Him By His Absence – 41
Days – 42
Practice for the Second Half of My Life – 44
Solstice – 45
In Another Lifetime – 46
The Great Beyond – 48
The World Collapses Here and Nothing Sails Beyond – 49

My Disaster – 51
Outing – 52
About Us – 54
The Return – 55
Wing Clipping – 56
The Roundabout – 57
In The Palms – 58
Left Between Us – 60

LIKE THIS FOR YEARS

One strung the beads and the other
undid the knot. Clickity went the flung

orbs and *hahaha* went our chortle.
We licked our hands, primordial.

We loved. An age old, time-worn,
truly dumb Whitman way. *Distance avails not.*

Lines we drove into each other's hearts.
Love between boobs and pigeon ribs,

the collision of cushion and pavement,
we pressed and prodded, relented

when dawn came, filled job orders,
splintered our path from the others,

scorned suburbs and stats
in banking, anything that sounded sure.

We were alive. For afternoons, filling in
our freckles with Sharpies. Dot lands.

Boy-woman, girl man, man boy, girl enough,
we tweaked our nipples, made pinch pots

of our asses. Pole-bending, fruit-opening
sex. God-wandering faith. Afternoons

spread in the sun of our bedroom.
Sheets and towels. Oh blow man,

tongue-boy, roof-creeper. Nose in the clavicle,
nose in the arse. Nose in the flowers. Nose in the stew.

We were two, a pair-some, sniffing like
snacking dogs, warbly line down the sidewalk,

each scent stringy as whiskey tits or goats.
Rubs, salves, flutter wind inside the gut,

fire enough for us, old stick and slot
we went and went, hotter than that

for years. Until the sky shook back
and rolled you up. No smell, no slackening

in the want, want —just the sun along
the bed-shore and me lying flat.

SPLIT SKY

Late afternoon in Marrakesh, a winter when the red
slows to orange and winds tingle the edges of palms
along the bled.
                       I'm inside the apartment
when the caller says *he's fallen* and I think of ice
which somebody will need later but I won't be the one.
There will be a lot of ice.
                     Ali Baba carpets
hung from the tops of houses, fly-away prayer
rugs and winds pushed by djinns. Little spirits spin
while I run to the Taxi.
                     I am running to the brim.
Under the black kettle wind, I come close to the well—
I'm stretching my arms to him like I'm pulling
a sweater overhead, his arms to my heart, heart
to my lungs, lungs
                     to my legs, the sheet,
the pavement, the doors thrown open, people
standing about, the onlookers from the balcony.
The world drops away and I'm shouting
and putting his coat around him. And his leg
up, knee bent.
                     Too heavy! I'm crying.
There was no end, no one could say it to me,
too big, that heart. Cluck of skin and muscle,
thump. Slur. After it stops for a few hours,
they plunk it into a tub. Organs go somewhere.

His stayed in Marrakesh, and the shell of him
came with me, home.
                              Formaldehyde and salt,
falling from the bone. Just the carry-carry coffin
we take overseas while the ocean sweeps
underneath and the calm is not calm but a capsule
of airline cabin, ding-ding goes the service bell,
whoosh the air along the portholes and soot collects
stopping up the engines, flushing through to the other side.

SEEING IS BELIEVING

Since your face is looking at the sky,
your eyes filming in, losing their sheen,
I don't see. I don't see.
I wrap myself in looking. I'm sheathed

in skin and can't reach you. My hands
wipe your cheek; the side of my face splinters,
craving skin on skin, how I'd tuck myself
into your neck: fuzz, stubble, warm.
Out there on the cement, I straighten your leg.
I make you into a corpse.
I fold your hands. It is all I know to do.
I put your sweet hands across you.

INTO THE BOX

When they put you into the box, you are thinner
than you'd been, and formaldehyde wells in your ears.
One eye wouldn't quite close. There are no stitches
to pull your lips together, no make-up and you
are beautiful. It is as you'd been, stopped there,
lit like the belly of a soft animal, flush within.
We are outdoors, sunlit. And it shone.
They wheel you out in the box. I come to you alone.
I stand while the men in butchers' blouses waited.
They wear gloves, latex ones. Sand-chunked stucco
of the courtyard. Windows shuttered.
Birds flicker under the huff of engines across the way.
They leave me alone with you.
I walk around you in the box. I see both sides.
They've put your prettiest cheek towards me, your right one,
and when I come around things look
off kilter. Your head lost bone and blood.
They've gently put a shower cap over your hair.
At the end, or what I think is the end, you whisper me
back to the box. It will be my last time before they seal it.
International law. I'm not supposed to be alone with you.
But I am and I want, in that space, to go and not go.
It is the last time I see your face, your hands,
you are in the djellaba, your face is next to mine.
My own face and your face. Our skin the same as the walls
along the medina, walled in city across the boulevard.
Don't be afraid. Now you have nothing to be afraid of,

I can hear this from you, drifting into me, out
into the square of the courtyard. I am trying to get away
and to get towards. So many things crowd
a person and then free her. Your face is skyward. Outside!
Just as you would love it. Would, would. And I turn back,
a few more minutes with you. I am next to your box again
and what I wouldn't give to be there again,
in that moment when I'm thinking,
I'll always remember this. Am I inside this moment still?
From your box in the medina, to the boulevards, to the hinterland.
To riverbeds dried ochre and crimson where other widows
in white scarves scrub clothes. Your pale glow ascends.
I'll be on the train, a slow clatter:
windows filthy, corridors and slapping doors
clacking like in the movies, only it won't be the movies,
a real train instead, the one I'll be on, taking you home
in the box, from the bled, to the bled and box, and back again.

MY DIFFICULT HOME

Even in the sunshine, the garbled heat of noon, when I leave
you there in your box, I can't get over when I leave

what I'll depart from: my husband, dear one, the man who raised me,
sweet, lanky, thin-shouldered dream. When I leave

Marrakesh, where scooters whir and donkeys strain and people believe
in reds, ochre, orange and pink, I'll remember when I leave:

We came to this. Me alive and you in the box. Our daughter pleading
for relief. Lavender lining, that box you lay in when I leave.

My face looks to the ground. Your face is skyward, not breathing
and they close the box. Who will turn to you when I leave?

Why this poem, Frances, to bury your dead? To have him every
place you go, but less, oh suffocating, smothering less, when you leave?

SLIGHT, THEN SWOON

Hands, your hands were your hands.
And the cheeks, they were your cheeks.
Still now, they are not. I press your hands,
wipe your cheek, set your skin in my palm.
It would rot away, it would not keep.

Fledgling soul, slipped-by man, your sleep
Was your sleep, your eyes were your eyes.
And they deflate, those rounds, as I keep
the brown turn of them; I make a place
inside my own—my eyes closed your eyes.

Your head, it was not your own. Your face,
I see it with the eyes now closed, once balm
to my ache, chin and forehead— no trace
of you in the midst of it. The horrible skull
I called my own, my head was not my calm

shore, just a mast-head, perched on the hull
of my body. My legs were your legs, the ones
I rubbed and longed for, the arms that lulled
and steadied me. My arms were your arms
and my legs, yours— the ones that could not run.

My body folded in, into your own—
breath missing, the embalming, drained and bled,
the mind taken, lungs deflated, skin-bones,

heart gutted, eyelids almost shut, faulty
arms that could not reach, so much still ahead.

A heart does not grow from flowers,
nor does the seam-on-seam of lovemaking
all those years console me in these hours.
One bloom will not become a vault
of perfume, nor the ashes one could shake

throughout the living room. Or the skin
inside a coffin, your own dear tendons
shivering to bone: a bled out skim
of who you were. I am skin and water.
How did we come apart, dear one?

THE LILT, THE TOPPLING OVER

Look, a sandwich. I'm eating it.
I pick it up and put it down.
And then: Here is a car.
I fold my legs into it,
pull the wheel to my chest.
Farther, there is a shop.
There will be reason to speak.
Think of a seizure.
Between gasps, just flashes.
I pressed the sandwich
to the roof of my mouth.
I touched the car's velvet
ceiling. Up ceiling.
I'm underneath. I keep it up.

THE BLED

Some passionate gospeller, some high energy missionary
in the desert could find Spiritus Mundi or the vast and
trunkless mass of disintegrating saints in the oracles
we visit and awaken from. God is God is god:
rough beast the rapture promises, shepherd who releases
virgins, king who offers keys to heaven's lock-up.
Christians and Muslims who pray for kingdoms to fall,
sand-tongued fate mongers, taunt the horizon's promise:
sanguine city and sky spread to murk under the dust
from burnt things. They await the raw animal.

Our desert flattens between the D'jibblets, little mountains,
and the great Atlas. How did we come to adore the bled?
Drain and suck of such a place, mat where Europe
dumps goods that lasted not a week, where goats eat
plastic bags, nudging scraps and their innards wrap
upon themselves, cruel knots caught until even
goats cannot heal. Where Sheep give birth and drag
bloodied lambs. One could see the frozen, scalded acre,
flashed with heat and cold, the brick-chunked
rocks on the cusp of sand, the not-so-far Sahara.

We live here. A family transplanted from the damp
moss and dark of America's northwest into the heat,
our rooms opening to the derbs in the medina,
old city, and out to the hinterlands. The air:
bled-tinged with smoke or cumin, oranges and the sights:

watchful farmers, wagon pullers and women wearing
red and orange skirts and torn sandals, pumping water.
Artichokes blooming thorny stars and bougainvilleas
splattering. Pomegranate trees flowering red, chard
going scarlet in the ground. It became our home,

near the scrimmage of sheep and the man who baked
cinderblocks with sand and ash, forming
his house from the bled. Alongside, the wrinkles of
would-be rivers—Lethe, Hades, Tensift— dry into beds.
Soot pocks the throat—stench pulls the stomach.
How my husband loved the place, goat paths
wobbling through sage and stone, how he followed them
home. To the men along the bled, tending sheep
making blocks, he'd waved. The air was dry and his
thirst took hold: "What is water but the generated soul?"

My husband's organs: dumped and burned in the bled.
Heart, kidney, liver, spleen deflated and cindered
under the little minaret speakers, the calls to prayer.
All shade is tin under this heat. My daughter and I
crawled along our breath; we touched the slowest parts
of hours and days, pawing toward the beast, hunger for
blood to flow, red and warm, for the slathering wet
to bathe us. What is water but the wizened well?
We prayed for him to cross the bled and crush the sphinx,
The terrible chunking of it against the horizon's spin—

WINGS INSTALLED

The pretty wing donor comes to see us.
Our surgeon spreads out his scalpels and fillet knives,
lines the bed in plastic wrap and puts us face flat.

We tuck our bellies, press our fists and wait

for medication to drop from our brains down
the ropes of our spines. Our shoulder blades poke up,
umbrellas unwrapped. Snap.

We lift the wings—switchblades— opening feathers
from our shoulders. Wing lady smiles and pats our hair.

Next, we're sliding pills down our throats,
our backs are singed along the wing slits,
where sutures and feathers pinch together.

We sleep with our cheeks to the pads.
We aren't machines and believe in transplants,
not tattoos or ornaments.

We wanted wings, not some parlor trick
or costume shop slip-ons, tulle bound on wire.
We had the ache for extra ligaments.

DYING IN THREE LANGUAGES

1.
I give you sun, sun through a blister.
That day had no evening or morning—it shrieked
and stayed. The mouth of afternoon yawned
and we saw teeth. That eye would not close.
The blood was bled. Shroud and scrim, the scarf's
gauze set the waking hour, unfurled the doom
I'd know on and on and would never outwit,
despite my tricks to lift him from the cement.

Rock-crushing gasp, pavement slammed,
basket roiling, metal screeching, planks
tumbling, cart thundering, car roaring.
Allah, oh *Allah*, is it day, is it night, better to pray
than to sleep, perchance to awaken within
slow motion lovers of this fast-trip derailleur?

The boy, with me when I come upon him,
slackens in the chest and he's pulled back.
In the scald of sunlight, the de-oranged
blanching of burnt white, our wills let go of our faces.

2.
My husband dies here, in North Africa,
playing basketball. He falls and his head caves in.
A man calls me and then a woman,
« Il est tombé. Viens, maintenant. »

I am looking for my shoes, his jacket, something to warm
or cool his knee. I tell the math tutor that it's no day
to be dressed for tragedy on the court and I'm laughing.
The tutor, nice Muslim man, is wincing a little but I know
the knee is the cause of Gary's falls, seamed and stitched, the one
that kept him from Viet Nam. Class of '69, front line.
The basketball rip. He played on it, and played—
king of the outside shot all these years and so again,
his leg must have given way.

I must be getting scared because I am grabbing things
and going to look for a taxi. I call my friend Ahmed and he's coming
but he takes a long time and Mehdi, his boy, is with me and we go
out to the big road, the one to Casablanca, Route de Casa,
look and look and a woman calls my phone this time—
he's fallen, he's fallen come now, and then Ahmed pulls up
and we go, the boy and me.
Then there are gates where the men stand around. One woman,
the one who called, disappears. Somewhere, I come in.
I'm running and I look to the offices, the mud walls dried pink, paint
layering off, a corridor outdoors and then he isn't there
not with an icepack putting up his knee. He isn't in there.
I am here now, writing this, instead at the table, my pen scratching
along yellow sheets. And the chest, my breath comes as if
from a jar, a sticky boiled up mass, not the deep, cool-in-the-valley
air of those out for a morning walk. Not the air of Ourika or Setti Fatma,
or the little clusters of mud-straw-ochre with tile or tin, sheds not huts:
the measure of second and third world, and the sway between them,
air along the paths where women carry loads of sticks
on their backs, along the riverbed, pink in the gravel,

us walking too, in worlds we cannot cross, we put out a finger and
can't reach the other but we can breathe the air,
we can breathe it. And I search the row, looking for a tall red-haired man
with his knee on a chair.

3.
My husband's body left from Casablanca.
Do we not ask, do we not speculate
what would he have said? Our flimsy
construction of him barely holding up.
And really he was in a box, in a truck
traveling through town by town,
permission granted, salute and stamp,
papers approved by state and embassy,
staving off decay in this Islamic county
where the dead, Gary that is,
belonged already in the ground.

His jacket went with him in the wagon,
late 1970's Renault, windows painted with white latex,
glass visible through the brush strokes;
I tucked the jacket next to his neck.
And I went by car to the police station,
and over and over I went to the police station.
Would the jacket keep him warm?
I pushed it like a pillow, I balled it up next to him.
They burned the place after him,
lit the blood where his head had come apart.
The scorch remained on the court.

4.
Our daughter and I walk behind the box.
My husband is in there, with a shower cap over his hair,
and he's wearing the djellaba that Abtef, dear Abtef, gave him.

In the aisle, we smooth our pace through the church
and onlookers practice the art of being human.
To see such glimpses of a grief, the crust of it, they'll live
into answers. For Maddy and me, we live along utterance.

I can never get it right. We have no spirit left for flinch.
The gloat and putter of a world humming on, sway and damage
of upright animals. Enough. He fell his way out and I feel my way out,

my ghost soldier in the windless box, my moon-skinned man
in high top sneakers, enormous bins for his feet
tucked inside the box.

5.
I turn upside down so the tears run over my forehead.
We imagine upwards. Burying down, but dreaming up.
Descent conjures sky. Solace. Scratch.
Older, older, to grow older and see the grandiose world,
the bitten promises — some people have less than this.
In my own daytimes, the heart is a room
that the mind can only visit.
I awaken to enclosures and build more.
He is the stuffing between all things.

I SHOULD SAY

A few words about basketball:
Age doesn't let it end well.

THREE WAYS OF LONGING

Three of us, standing in our pajamas.
The house empty and a suitcase on the hearth.
Then there are two.

One suitcase holds most things:
letters, photographs, books and dresses.
We wonder how to re-fold them.

"If I had to pick one of you," my daughter says,
"I'd pick you." And that's good, I guess,
because I'm the one she has left.

KINSHIP

We stretched our feathers
over each other, and then
across the foundling child.
She was without. No wings,
not from where she came.
We took her in and made
her part of this world without
loft and cloud. We crawled
up on either side of her;
we spread our wings
tip to tip and tucked the girl's
little face beneath.
Amidst the humming
song of the hand-cranked,
cable-round-the-gear,
squeak and thimble melody,
we winged her: fragile girl,
beloved child. Ours.

TRIO DOWN ONE

We flagged the moon, June-boy,
to no song's avail. Trusty locker
where we put our things; then
fortune dropper,
we steered to the seas.

Come back. Retrieve the goods,
pull us from the rubble
boy-bug, lover-smush,
daddy-right. Tell me
that cemetery isn't real.

Promise me you are late
from work. A few notes and
the whole song goes *whish*—
we flutter cordless, shoeless,
through some ache-land

where we left our things
strewn here and there,
chairs and adding machines
in the desert, mud clumps drying.
Keys with dust and legs unhinged.

Goats ate; we starved.
Fate stopper, you're not
home yet. Ship's in port.
Hear that calcium
scrape along the rails of our stay?

CONSOLE, PREACHER, CONSOLE

God has him now, a lady said
and I said, "Well I want him back."
My husband needs shoes.
Right now our nephew is wearing
the old ones to paint the deck.
Soles flopping. Wherever God
has him now is not like here
where I can't keep anything straight—
the sun is always in my eyes and someone's
got an engine running for God's sake,
sounds of pipes bursting and flooding,
like the backseat ride of a car gone
wild through the Tangier headlands, over the sea
no end in sight, just wrap and flip between
cliff and inland. A couple sent
notice of their payment to a whole abbey
where monks are chanting my dear one's name
over and over, calling to the God who took him,
the one who has him now.
In some pre-literate daze, t-clucked tingles,
throat static, the monks push their chapel
skyward, hoping to conjure him up
when they didn't know him.
But I did and he needs shoes.
As if prayers or footwear might prevent
the ripping poison in some artery or aneurism
or rogue bone chip sailing into his brain,

knocking him
dead to the world, to the ground plain and simple,
Or the fact that the pavement tipped,
God's prison upended, and that was it.

PROBLEMS WITH CLOTHES

Around a wing, a blouse needs folds.
Tailors slice our seams and put in zippers

opening the pleats. Even so,
Our wings flicker, humped under clothes.

Twitching skin and sinew, we squeeze
and rub. Raw bumps where ointments fail.

We tug at garments, worry the hems
under our thumbs and soil them.

On and off they go, these body rags;
scents come loose, they agitate in soap.

Clothes-pinned to the rope, our shirts
lift in the wind. They dry cartoon-thin—

Our wings too full for them.

PINNING ON WINGS

In a world gone by with tear-downs and believers who
stole everything from the land, propped up flim-flam
condominiums and sold us plastic dreams, who rolled
super stores into the meadows and shoved chemicals
into streams, we were nearly birds,
floating along the crusts of pavement and broken tin.

Amidst the Arabs we roamed, a sunburnt twosome,
beyond the district's edge. Plastic choked the goats
and sheep; donkeys honked with thirst and dirt singed
our nostrils; the river stained red the land and nudged
smoke into the palms. In the bled, we almost belonged,
swerving along the sheep paths. Perhaps the Berbers
thought us French in our pinkness, in our white socks:
two people who'd pasted on wings, wilting in the heat.

It's how it felt, near the end. All the scorch and rocks,
thirst and donkeys, carts and oranges, cumin, artichokes
blooming in chunked-up land. Burning tar, riverbed
sewage. Breathing it in. Hating the Europeans for sucking
water out of the desert and flooding their golf courses,
for scoffing at the poor, for taking good money away,
north across the straits. We huffed underneath our wings,
took scalding routes to the *hanouts*, little shops in the walls,
bought almonds and soda. Our ligaments quivered open:
twitching when we spoke or when we waved along the bled.

For awhile, we dropped feathers.
We wore airfoils and pulled at threads.

Wings, from a distance, are eyelashes.
I could see him, barely, wisp on the outcropping.
He walked and walked, shading his eyes — never a hat,
never sunglasses — He walked from a grave inside out.
I missed something and stopped. He kept walking into
the land of neither: the land we'd come to, the land of home,
both the beyond and here. I couldn't catch up to him;
I reached for his wings. I saw them flicker and lift, the sway of
feathers and wind; the djinns of seven p.m. took over again,
sucked the flown from whatever flew and clutched
his wings caught in the closing, or maybe the wind
shutting down, and he lay upon them at his sunlit stop.

AFTER THE BLED, ON TO THE SHOALS

Over and around,
tucked in the muck-soaked boots
clucking sludge in the fen, skunk cabbage
up the peat black croak.

Pressed under
sky-knuckles, clouds knocked about
rock outcroppings, branches
thumbing thistles and nettles.

Torn-up things
float inside the skin, flip
within organ space.
Spleen tumble, stomach spin.

Look up.
Hills flit under the mist cover,
needle trees shag the grey
green, green, dark then.

Blue goes the sky.
Flop open the diary, tug
arms from the sweater twisted up:
inside-out, clutch the seams you can see.

THE PATIENT SAINT

I know I have a body.
In this bone tangle, heart
wrung from the dropped
hearth of ribs, caught in
fireworn wrangles of ash
brought back. No Eve
am I, just flesh sent
a long way, intact.

From inside, my body caves
to wrapped marrow—
joint and splint. What
place of rich winds,
spin and flinch
of blood-culled gutterways
brings this desert—
skull, mites like
lichened fossils? A mote's
slow drop into a river
bile and brine,
twined to rib and bone?

Cold outside, my cage
fires within though
I'm slow to fist,
quick in blood gone thin.
I'm counting: white, red, white.

Fringe dust and spores,
washed edges of a ravine
dropping nonetheless
into the sea. Silt, slough
the residue of salts
or some other. Wither.

IN THE SPACE

Left by the body,
we try and fill in—dinner steams,
the place settings—three—
one shiny plate still clean.
The chair once nudged,
conversation's rope
gone slack,
space we don't use up,
shoes tidied in rows,
the bed, cold to one side.
Agony: shafts up the body
igniting the pilot,
filling up the balloons of our chests.
Doors of comings and goings:
we walk through upright
rectangles, narrow boxes.

YOU COULD KNOW HIM BY HIS ABSENCE

Do not lean out windows over the
wishes of others
Do not look into the crowd that roars
for the dictator
Do not slide into a world built on
ego and riches

and think you will find my husband.

DAYS

My dear one's leg, I dreamed, is buried in my back.
I awaken to the heaviness, and the weak carriage that
ribs can be, and shoulders. Wagon-load,
love-sprung cart of whatever I can hold.

Here's the stack of shirts. There are the shoes.
Once, everything sheathed the body that held him.
Does it come back to me? I wear the shirts.
I plant flowers in the shoes. Dead man's lace-ups

lumbering, and the pinch of his thigh and knee
across my neck. I carry the sweet bird stretch
of him, pulling my dead friend along, packed up.
I lean into the wind; I reach back.

Only he can't be dead. That's some night's sleep,
terror unglued from the theater set in my ribs.
I wait, and the awake doesn't come. I will scream.
It was a slippage. He went sideways

for a moment, slammed his head; they took him away,
in the wagon, in the morgue, then into the box,
the planes, the cargo holds, the trucks, the church,
the cemetery, the shaft, the dirt

and we went off without him. But the zing of our hearts,
hands we held, shoulders we fit inside and laid across

each other's — I felt them still. Space that held.
Air that stayed. Chair that froze

his outline. Plates in the dish rack, tagine on the stove.
Things remained. All those years together become *once
upon a time* — his voice turned around and went
inside me: he wore the shirts, tied the shoes,

zipped the coat. These things stay. I have the shriek
across my back. When they thread his stiffened arms
into the djellaba and put a cap across his head,
right then, our strange new relationship begins.

PRACTICE FOR THE SECOND HALF OF MY LIFE

Lentement, mon ami, mon amour, je suis. Mais ici.

A suitable bedding, a suitable garment, a suitable walk outside.
A suitable thump of the hand, swivel of the shoulder.
A suitable egg.

Thunder from my clothing. Shriek from the frame of the bed.
So much muscle and talk, so much climb and sway.

And, in the yellow kitchen:
One Gerber daisy, pink,
bending away.

SOLSTICE

I will my dreams to find him. I will my shoes to cover
my feet. I will the haircut, the end of the movie.
I will my man with a stiffening nubbin to hug me.
I will his chest to me. I will my hair across his ribs.
Ladles and pans for the soup kitchens. I will the podium,
the pillow, the steering wheel. I will the poems and
him sleeping next to me. I will the old underwear,
the chilled airport. Back to us. I will the robe:
our friend Abtef's djellaba. I will bandshells and accordions;
I fade towards earth, I will him back. I will him
at each moment when I fail and Maddy fails and we love
and I will

IN ANOTHER LIFETIME

He'd come back and I wouldn't recognize him
doing all those things
he once refused: hiking uphill for the view,
swimming (head
under) and going to plays. He declined, in the end,
bicycles, fish, chopsticks,
doormats, ice skates, cocktail parties and blue jeans.
He put off singing
Christmas carols, skiing, tipping his shoes in puddles.
My just-gone lover,
dee-jay, house rocker whisked into lands of flutter,
splints and whispers
huge in outer space. He's dissolving in clouds that move
away from dirt
wafting apricots and almonds, oils, silks and leather.
God is swabbed
in sweat. Allah-blessed, the Amizigh women sell
wool hats, ones
he bought on hot, hot days in Marrakesh. Without him,
places aren't much.
Ground and sky. And air. Separate realms, no end to them.
No secret plan—
He'd simply find a way to come to us again. This consoles:
the way he sits,
his back to me, and turns, lips plumped with lipstick.
Returning stranger
and stranger, he shows up: my own limbs lightening

with each new greeting—
a man who never washed his cheeks: the scruff,
fleece against my face.

THE GREAT BEYOND

Of course there is my hunger for messages.
The chop-chop of loneliness—
an egg, the orbed perfection of it
on the yellow countertop.
His blue shorts, the grey cement.
The brick and salt of it, the crust of it,
feed bin and charcoal of it,
the bled of it, stench of it, lag and sway
of it. Skin burn and chill of it, the sun of it.
Someone lied about the universe.
All of it a clench.
Release does not come.
Going back is an undoing.
Things were clear and seeded.
Cropped and tended. Sewn.

THE WORLD COLLAPSES HERE
AND NOTHING SAILS BEYOND

Old masters, men who passed years at the hearth,
roamed the gallery where they faced brush-wipings,
squinted at Camera Lucida portraits,
who wandered almost empty airports and saw
February's windows glisten and vent-ways steam,
I am not like them. Museums must wait,
the civic spaces of commerce and din,
my husband is dead.
I am not masterful or old, and my child has no
living other. We see his box, long cedar,
up the ramp, into the belly of the plane.
Far-off, where we'll go, a river flushes cold,
rock cold into hills, while here in chutes of glass
we pass our living selves.

The old themes run slow, while the verse of our age
clogs before love and grief, attention fixed to syntactic
clatter and the disguise of old dreams amidst the shining
ruins. *They had changed their throats and had the throats
of birds.* My husband brings me upright from sleep—
we bend, night by night, to the shovel,
to the clay. Our hands are dirty,
callused and hovering, at the dinner table.
Centuries bled inside us, drying to rouge
and red to earth salt, flagging beauty
from drainage. We learned that here, in this ruddy land.

We take him home. The two of us: girl and woman,
our gasps pinched in our hearts, breath gone to dust,
in between worlds, dizzy with it.
Mostly, I'm breathing the top of the air.
I'm sucking the skim off. An animal peeling back
the flesh, snarling through the bones for her cub—
the gasp and look, her eyes horrified, waiting for it
in the hunger of all things it could bring.

MY DISASTER

Lost a glove, lost the wallet, then it grew
into the brown jacket, the way back home,
childhood photographs, then you

lost your life. People removed
you from their lists. I hovered over
your terrible absence, the fluke

swept into a mysterious, red world
where donkeys worked without water.
Along that edge, near the wall, unfurled

our half-built city and the ancient ruse
of shelter: fronds over tin, slaughter
pens for sheep, garbage strewn

through the desert, derbs that curled
into the medina—places I can't get to.
The loss masters me; it's an art, the pearl

I can't admire. Our keys have fallen into
the outflow pipe; the red city we loved
mastered our wits, our breath. Then you.
Right it. Right it, I keep saying, *my disaster.*

OUTING

Today, I go to the cemetery
and lie upon the grave.
When I tip my head back
it was as if I tipped your head back.
We press upon the little stone—
last name and first initial—
G. Greaves.
 With a marker, I write:
I. Grieve.

I let my body sink
into the grass. The
moon a mushy skull
inside a rainy sky.
My fever reddens. Mist gathers
the round-wets spilling
until the salt of flesh
and rivulets—
goes brackish

at the mouth—
water catches and I stay still.
Plane overhead, a shaft
with a red blotch
like a missile carrying
blood through the grey,
an ache. The rain makes no

sound upon my face.
I smell your tiredness
after work—
long days pushing
brooms and sanders,
cleaning fluids and you
sloughing it off but the wet stuff
stays on me. And there's
this problem with
my arms and legs,
with my torso,
shoulders and neck, the way
I'm all body and you are all spirit.
There is no
hulk, no portion of you. No other.
I'm a crust. Water flecks.

Say I'm the dead
one and you are lying here
under the sky where it's not
quite dark. Almost.
I can hear the graves
shifting, all of your people
underground in catacombs
and cement. As if I took x-rays.
The tombs move.
On top, I freeze
in the rain's massive bloom.

ABOUT US

Each day I wait for ten o'clock
then one-thirty and after that
four. O, o, o'clock. I wait.
You will fly from your box
deep in the hill nearby,
the box hand-built in our far-off
city. You'll lift up, take
to your feet, lean over the drawer
in our daughter's room
and pull it open.
I'll be just in back of you, watching
for your hands upon those wings—
mother of pearl
feathers, dark and fresh,
some green and then blue.

THE RETURN

Sometime later, I went back
to that part of Marrakesh—
bougainvillea walls and
orange trees, djinns in
early evenings, shade.
My daughter wouldn't go
to that place where
her dad fell.
I did, and there I saw the man
who minds the gates. He said
Hello and nodded. But he wasn't
warm. There was language
between us. We both had more words
than we admitted. I have some
Derija, and he has some French
but we left our encounter to nodding
and *Ssalâmo ʒalîkom*. Peace upon you.
And Peace upon you,
in return. He'd turned formal—
I was bad luck, de-flowered,
a version of the wind
blowing through a woman
that a widow is.

WING CLIPPING

Once, wings lifted our little imaginings skyward,
Icarus engines:
chug-whiffs. Umbrellas, too, flicked— round upon the streets—
puff-snap blooms.
We did not go aloft, but flight was looming in our crusted eyes.

Only wreckage now. We're clutching feathers and singing,
our landing gear
trimmed and in our line of vision: bled out there, bled within.

THE ROUNDABOUT

Sheep, goats, a man with a coat of unplucked geese
across his djellaba pleats. Spread wings,
stiffened at his hips, tipping in the steam
and wind. If feathers could lift him,
curve his shoulders over the scooter smoke,
he'd drift above the hammam stacks
where sweat slows to musk,
sanded from skin, the smell of rope.
But the motos shriek along the wall,
slant into the roundabout— around
boys with donkeys, men in trucks,
stay clear! a bus, three wooden fruit wagons,
woman on crutches and the autos.
He inhales the two-stroke engine mist,
taxi beeps and men yelling to the beasts.
Clop-clop next to this, next to that:
at the hurry-hurry crossroads, more bloom
than dust, the go go go 'round in his robe
with the geese, sandaled feet— off to hearth
and grill, flight grounded, moving still.

IN THE PALMS

A wall surrounds the city, this red place
of dust and carts and oranges and tombs
made from desert sand:
ochre, brown, almost salmon—the color of your hair,
and your freckles, that same brown of the dirt
people press smooth with their feet.
The wall is mud and hay formed upright
a thousand years old.

On your last day, we followed you to the old city,
where the wall wrapped around
alleys and palms. We followed as you stepped through
a door in the wall, a person-sized keyhole.
We were three keys, one, two, three.

Sleep comes in between things.
Night arcs through us, whipping your ochre,
your browns, your reds back to us.
As though we are touching your cheeks,
as though the wind could console.

Ahead of us, you walk to find out.
We try to follow you.
There is no city like the one we keep.
"We're here," we call, "We're here."

But you've smiled and turned on
a road swollen to the horizon
and us here, we're pointing, still waving.

LEFT BETWEEN US

I was caught underground too, under there.
Growing things, roots and worms, how lovely it was.
Through my throat, the tangle of vines, how fresh,
how at home I grew. The sniff of moss, the froth
underneath, rot baggy, root-dangles

in the green, the bloody green, green of it,
willow switch and the leaf's clingy drip,
the fabric forest of it. There I was, as the flesh of
bud and rope, of stem and stone and earth.
I became the dirt— coddled and stuffed.

Cold. As my sweet companion is. As the plant
stemming through my nose and mouth,
vines in the sinus, buds caught in the passages,
another mortuary I am growing into:
seedling and root. I am growing used to it.

When the night shifts and lifts me through the soil,
when the orange city light peeks through the seam,
I am pawing dirt. Chilled. My night-time view,
the one above the earth. Coddled turf, green
and glistening, rummaging fleck by fleck,

I'm stretched in the moist dark. Up against
the clammy him, the box the only thing between us,
splintering, sagging wood, coming apart.
And we are merging. I feel the tingle of it.

NOTES

Djinns are the little spirits said to occupy a world in parallel to our own.

From "Practice for the Second Half of My Life," the translation of *Lentement, mon ami, mon amour, je suis. Mais ici* : Slowly, my friend, my love, I am. But here.

"The World Collapses Here and Nothing Sails Beyond" owes airports to Auden and "the throats of birds" and "What's water but the generated soul?" to Yeats.

"The Patient Saint" appeared in *Cutbank*.

FRANCES MCCUE is a poet and prose writer who lives in Seattle with her daughter Madeleine Greaves. Her husband, Gary Greaves, died on February 12, 2009. A Public Scholar, McCue is Writer in Residence and Lecturer in the Honors Program at the University of Washington. From 1996 to 2006 she directed Seattle's Richard Hugo House, a literary center which she co-founded. She has been a Fulbright Senior Scholar, a Klingenstein Fellow, an Echoing Green Fellow and a winner of the Barnard New Women Poets Prize. Her work has been supported by Artist Trust, 4 Culture, Seattle Arts Commission and Hedgebrook. Beacon Press published *The Stenographer's Breakfast*, her first book of poems. In 2010, her book about Richard Hugo and Northwest towns, *The Car That Brought You Here Still Runs*, came out from the University of Washington Press.

FACTORY
HOLLOW
PRESS

Amherst
Massachusetts